Talking with Evang...

A Guide for Catholics

Ralph Del Colle

PAULIST PRESS
New York / Mahwah, NJ

Cover and book design by Lynn Else

Library of Congress Cataloging-in-Publication Data

Del Colle, Ralph.
Talking with evangelicals : a guide for Catholics / Ralph Del Colle.
    p. cm.
  Includes bibliographical references (p.   ).
  ISBN 978-0-8091-4742-7 (alk. paper)
  1. Catholic Church—Relations—Evangelicalism. 2. Evangelicalism—Relations—Catholic Church. I. Title.
  BR1641.C37D45 2012
  280′.042—dc23

                               2011035378

Published by Paulist Press
997 Macarthur Boulevard
Mahwah, New Jersey 07430

www.paulistpress.com

Printed and bound in the
United States of America

Table of Contents

Introduction

When a Catholic encounters a conservative Evangelical Protestant for the first time it makes at the very least for an interesting conversation. Usually, the Catholic is taken for a loss, not knowing quite how to answer questions such as:

> Are you saved?
> Have you been born again?
> Do you know Jesus Christ as your personal
>   Lord and Savior?

If the encounter continues, the Catholic may soon discover that the Evangelical is quite familiar with the Bible, is able to quote it at will, and may even challenge the Catholic to justify his or her beliefs and practices in its light. Catholic appeals to tradition do not persuade the Evangelical, since tradition is judged to be merely human in origin compared to the divine inspiration of Holy Scripture.

Is it even possible for this conversation to continue? Does it have to break off with two fellow Christians from different traditions passing like ships in the night, speaking different theological languages in two very incompatible religious worlds? It is the purpose of this book to encourage the possibilities of Catholic-Evangelical dialogue in a peaceful, charitable, and ecumenical spirit. We share a common witness to our faith in Jesus Christ, even in the diversity and distinctiveness of our two Christian traditions.

This short volume will be divided into two parts in order to effectively introduce Catholics to the Evangelical world (part one) and facilitate interaction with Evangelicals by Catholic Christians (part two).

PART I

What Is an Evangelical Christian?

We begin with a brief introduction of the Protestant Evangelical world for Catholics. Often the term is used in association with Fundamentalism, which in most circles possesses a rather negative connotation. The two terms are indeed related but are distinguished both by those who use them as self-designations and by scholars who study them. One shorthand formula is to remember that Evangelicalism historically has its roots in Fundamentalism and that Fundamentalism is but one segment of the contemporary Evangelical movement. We will begin with Fundamentalism after providing some important historical and theological background.

North American Protestantism from the eighteenth century on was always strongly Evangelical. The word *evangelical* comes from *evangel* (*evangelium* in Greek) or *Gospel*, that is, "good news." In itself the word is not unfamiliar to Catholics. We speak, for example, of the evangelical counsels of poverty, chastity, and obedience, which men and women religious observe. The connection is with Jesus and the good news or Gospel that he proclaimed and, which he himself is, through the saving mystery of his death and resurrection. The Easter Triduum is the annual celebration of the good news of this paschal mystery. During the Reformation the Protestant Reformers understood their efforts as a return to the Gospel, or evangel. Their "protest" was in their view an Evangelical confession (i.e., a Gospel confession) of the Christian faith over against the abuses of belief and practice that they perceived in the Catholic Church.

Two important Reformation principles are significant for any contemporary understanding of Fundamentalism and Evangelicalism: First, Holy Scripture or the Bible was the only authority that the Reformers recognized and by which they sought to ground their doctrines or beliefs. *Sola scriptura*, "Scripture alone," was the basis for the new Protestant faith. For the most part this either qualified or entirely ruled out the role of church tradition and pastoral office (such as the pope and bishops) as authorities for Christian doctrine and practice.

Second, the Reformers were concerned with the issue of how one was saved. It was Martin Luther who asked the question: "How can I find a gracious God?" The answer was the doctrine of justification by faith, that is, being made righteous before God through faith in Jesus Christ. Salvation is a free gift offered to all who trust Christ for their righteousness. Initially, this excludes good works. Good works are evidence of justifying faith but they don't count toward it. Sanctification or holiness is a fruit of justification, not part and parcel of it as in Catholicism, where faith combines with the works of love to make one holy, to become actually righteous. For Protestants one is declared righteous because of Christ's work for us. Faith accepts this and holiness follows. Hence there are two important Evangelical doctrines common to most Protestant traditions: The Bible alone is the basis of faith; and faith in Jesus Christ saves us from the consequences of sin, not any good work we might perform.

This basic Evangelical emphasis of the Reformation took a distinctive shape in the new world of North America, where many of the first English settlers were influenced by Puritanism, a more radically Protestant expression of faith as compared to many Anglicans, who preserved some Catholic elements in their tradition. Unlike their fellow Anglicans (the Puritans were nonconformists vis-à-vis established Anglicanism and, if they were Congregationalists or Separatists, they entirely dismissed the Church of England) the Puritans stressed that biblical precedent alone should govern the structure of the church as well as Christian teaching and worship.

Additionally, within Puritanism, heavily influenced as it was by Calvinism and its doctrine of predestination, the assurance of one's salvation became a most pressing concern. In other words, how does one know that God has chosen or elected one for salvation? The solution was found along two main tracks: First, the Puritans sought to confirm their faith by a holy lifestyle according to the law of God. If one was a

Christian, it should be evident in one's way of life. Popular impressions of Puritan strictness and severity have their origin here, although they were not the dour lot that is so often depicted. Second, some sought the confirmation in their Christian experience of God. That is, one could be aware of one's own conversion and that the grace of God is indeed operative in one's life. Since salvation was the crucial issue, this experience usually had to do with the sense that one's sins were forgiven, that the Holy Spirit had applied the work of Christ's saving death and resurrection to one's own life. It was an experience of regeneration (some of them called it "sealing," an experience that was more the assurance of regeneration than regeneration itself), and what contemporary Fundamentalists and Evangelicals call "being born again."

It was in this context that this broadly Evangelical tradition of dissenting North American Protestants (Remember the Pilgrims!) were impacted by revivalism during the First Great Awakening in the mid-eighteenth century. Simply put, revivalism intensified the quest for the assurance of salvation. Catholics must realize that this quest has everything to do with Evangelical theology. If salvation is a free gift offered to a person through faith, then the assurance of faith, that is, one's personal trust in Jesus Christ, becomes the object of concern. Revivalism tended to emphasize the crisis nature and affective dimension of this quest. It could happen in response to the words of the preacher. It could be highly emotional or simply be a quiet sense of God's presence as expressed by John Wesley, the founder of Methodism, when he exclaimed that his heart was strangely warmed.

Before the Civil War in the United States most of Protestant life was Evangelical in tone. No better expression of this sensibility exists than the traditional American folk hymn "Amazing Grace," the first stanza of which is familiar to nearly all: "Amazing grace, how sweet the sound that saved a wretch like me. / I once was lost but now am found, was blind but now I see."

Following the war there emerged certain distinctive Evangelical emphases that gave rise to modern Fundamentalism. In addition to revivalism, which focused on Evangelism (bringing people to Christ) and missions, there arose the holiness movement and other varieties of "higher life" movements that were intended to deepen the Christian life of believers. Also, prophecy conferences and *premillennialism*, which anticipated the end times and the imminent return of Christ, became popular. They often elaborated their expectations by setting out schemas for the fulfillment of Bible prophecy. Finally, the so-called Princeton theology—undertaken by Presbyterian theologians at Princeton Theological Seminary in New Jersey—presented sophisticated arguments to defend the inerrancy and infallibility of the scriptural text. The objective here was to reaffirm the authority of the Bible in an increasingly secular world. Remember,

"Scripture alone" was still the Protestant principle and norm of authority for the truth of Christian faith.

This rehearsal of Evangelical history is intended to alert the Catholic Christian to the variety that exists within the movement. Roughly, when encountering an Evangelical Christian, they will express either or both of these two major concerns. Their respect for the authority of Scripture and their witness to the saving power of Jesus Christ coalesce as the basic Evangelical expression of the faith. Some may emphasize the experiential dimension of conversion and holiness. Others will witness to the reliability of God's promises, including prophecy and the expectation of the last days. Still others will try to demonstrate the surety of the Bible, not only as it concerns the message of the Gospel but also its verity in matters of science and history. All will have a concern for Evangelism and mission and, despite many disagreements among themselves over matters of doctrine and practice, they do share a Bible- and Christ-centered faith.

An important factor to consider in the development of modern and contemporary Evangelicalism was the situation in American Protestantism during the latter portion of the nineteenth century. During this time the *historical-critical* method of biblical interpretation was introduced by mainstream Protestant scholars. For the first time, scholars began using linguistics, archeology, and other academic disciplines to understand the processes by which the books of the

Bible came to be written. Their discoveries led them to conclude that, in some cases, certain words may not have been spoken by biblical characters but may, in fact, have been written by an author or redactor (editor) of the final text. For example, a saying of Jesus in the Gospels may actually reflect the situation of the early church rather than the exact words of Jesus himself. Scholars also concluded that certain events in the Bible may not have happened precisely as they were described, or may have simply been literary devices for conveying spiritual ideas.

As many in the mainstream Protestant denominations began to assimilate historical-critical methods of biblical research and as the culture became more secular and less dominated by the Evangelical Protestant ethos, some Protestants began to critique these modernist and liberal trends. Protestants became divided between those who embraced the new way of looking at the Bible and those who preferred to believe that the Bible was literally true in every respect. At stake was the very reliability of the Bible in the face of historical and scientific criticism. The new theory of evolution, which put into question the historical validity of the Book of Genesis, played no small part in the debates.

On a cultural level, other changes were under way. Some Protestants were placing less faith in the possibilities of human progress; hence the acceptance of *premillennial* scenarios of fulfillments of biblical prophecy and the return of Christ. Specifically, this meant that after Christ's "second coming" (his *parousia* in theological language), he will reign for a thousand years on earth *before* the final judgment (hence "millennial"—see Rev 20:1–10). So, premillennialism posits that there will be a thousand-year reign of Christ on earth between his second coming and the final judgment:

Second Coming ⟶ Thousand Year Reign ⟶ Final Judgment

This contrasts with the earlier *postmillennial* view, also based on Revelation 20:1–10, that was common before the Civil War. According to the postmillennial view, the kingdom of God would be realized in church and society (a truly Christian civilization!) for a thousand years before the second coming of Christ, at which point all of creation would be consummated in the resurrection of the dead and the last judgment.

This postmillennial understanding of Christian eschatology had become a basis for much Christian activism in society. (Eschatology is the study of the last things: heaven, hell, resurrection of the dead, last judgment, and the consummation of the kingdom of God). The antislavery movement was a good example of this. Many abolitionists had strong postmillennial Evangelical convictions. If one believes that we can participate in building the kingdom of God, specifically the reign of Christ in the world, one will act much differently than those who held the later more pessimistic premillennial view. A premillennialist often expects that things in society will only get worse and then Christ will come to save the church from the evils of this world.[1] We shall return to the subject of eschatology below. Additionally, the concern for holiness in a more secular and worldly culture led many to form a subculture of Evangelical faith. Some even called for separation from the mainstream of American life.

Initially, those who waged the battle against the use of the historical-critical method in mainstream Protestantism (e.g., in the Presbyterian Church) called themselves *Fundamentalists*. They were professedly antimodernist and defended the fundamentals of the faith, usually grouped together as:

1. The inspiration and infallibility of the Bible
2. The deity of Jesus Christ and his virgin birth
3. The substitutionary atonement of Christ's death
4. His bodily resurrection
5. His second coming in glory

All of these ideas were either being disputed or being revised among theologians in mainstream Protestantism. After having lost the battles for control of their denominations in the 1920s, some Fundamentalists around the time of the Second World War attempted a different approach in their efforts to confess their faith. These people, more open to society and more intellectually engaged with modernity, became known as *neo-Evangelicals*, or today simply *Evangelicals*. What follows is a brief word about the differences between them and Fundamentalists before we proceed with some specific issues that arise in dialogue between Catholics and Evangelicals.

Fundamentalists are those Evangelical believers who hold most firmly to an inerrantist view of Scripture with respect to all aspects of human knowledge that the Bible touches upon, *including history and science*. For example, they consider it essential to defend the historicity of the story of Noah's ark as well as a creationist view of human origins, as opposed to an evolutionary perspective. If the Bible is in error on these matters, they argue, then one cannot trust its view on matters of faith and morals. At its beginning some sectors of the movement could be quite intellectually rigorous in their theology, as was the case with the "Princeton theologians" whom Fundamentalists sought as allies in their cause.

Fundamentalists also tend to be separatist, refusing to fellowship with other Christians who disagree with them. (In Evangelical and Fundamentalist circles, *fellowship* is commonly used as a verb to mean engaging in religious cooperation or shared worship with other Christians.) Some scholars distinguish between militant or closed Fundamentalists and moderate or open Fundamentalists. As the label suggests, the latter group is less separatist than the former, but both groups would largely reject accepted scholarly methods of biblical interpretation. On the other hand, moderates are more interested in a certain degree of academic respectability. In other words, the closed Fundamentalists are suspicious of most academic theology and would teach just "what the Bible says," whereas the open Fundamentalists attempt to support their theological positions with a degree of scholarly effort, even if they do not accept Christian theologies other than their own. They will also fellowship with Christians from other denominations even if they are not interested in any formal denominational connections with others. The closed Fundamentalists do not even go that far and may even refuse to fellowship with other Fundamentalists and Evangelicals whom they judge to have compromised the faith.

Evangelicals, on the other hand, have thoroughly engaged other Christians, accepted most scholarly theological and biblical methods, and rather than form a subculture, are attempting to interact with the wider culture. Some Evangelicals are progressive, others more conservative, but they would hold to the infallibility and authority of Scripture (with some still insisting on inerrancy) especially with regard to questions of faith, ethics, and doctrine. They still hold to the necessity for Evangelical conversion (that is, one's own saving encounter with Christ) and probably still affirm all the major fundamentals, but with a respectable and studied theological attitude.

One example of the differences between Fundamentalists and Evangelicals might be helpful. Both affirm the importance of the Christian hope in the second coming of Christ. But the Evangelicals do not hold to the elaborate prophetic schemes that Fundamentalists construct, such as the dispensational "regathering" of Israel in the Holy Land and the rapture of the church, in which God directs history in the light of his dispensations with Israel (to fulfill the prophecy of regathering) and the church (to save Christians from the tribulation that will afflict Israel by rapturing them into heaven before it begins).

All of this is to say that the Evangelical world is a rather large tent with a great deal of diversity inside of it. As far as Catholics are concerned our best dialogue partners are Evangelicals. Fundamentalists either are not interested because they militantly reject the Catholic Church as the great Harlot of the Book of Revelation or they have effectively passed into the Evangelical camp and are therefore engaged with other Christians and the culture at large. We conclude this section by quoting the characteristics of Evangelicalism proposed by a contemporary Evangelical theologian, with the reminder that Fundamentalists hold these as well within a much stricter and often anti-intellectual frame of mind. Mainstream Evangelicals consciously sought to avoid such a posture and therefore represent a much more intellectually credible presentation of Protestant Evangelical faith. The core Evangelical doctrines as articulated by theologian Richard Lints are:

1. Scripture has final authority.
2. God does his saving work in history.
3. Eternal salvation is possible only through the atoning death of Christ.
4. We receive salvation only through personal faith in Jesus Christ.
5. Evangelism and missions are critically important.
6. It is important to have a spiritually transformed life.[2]

As we shall now see, Catholics share much in common with this understanding of faith as some Evangelicals and Catholics have already witnessed to in dialogue. Two dialogues are worthy of mention.

First, from 1977 to 1984, the Secretariat for Promoting Christian Unity (now the Pontifical Council for Promoting Christian Unity) officially sponsored the Evangelical-Roman Catholic Dialogue on Mission. This dialogue was international in scope. Another round of that dialogue took place from 1993 to 2002 between the Pontifical Council and the World Evangelical Alliance (formerly the World Evangelical Fellowship) on the subject of "Church, Evangelization, and the Bonds of

Koinonia." In the United States in 1994, a consultation between Evangelicals and Catholics produced a common declaration entitled "Evangelicals and Catholics Together: The Christian Mission in the Third Millennium." This was not an official dialogue. On the Catholic side it was not sponsored by either the Vatican or the National Conference of Catholic Bishops (now the United States Conference of Catholic Bishops, which sponsored a dialogue with Evangelicals from 2003 to 2008 without producing a report). But the focus of this dialogue lent itself to the affirmation of moral concerns within the body politic of American culture. Needless to say, the more ecumenically significant of the two is the former, the Evangelical–Roman Catholic Dialogue on Mission, where serious theological issues were explored. The statement "Evangelicals and Catholics Together" (ECT) simply highlights the common front that Catholics and Evangelicals can form on certain moral issues in the public square. Later documents from "Evangelicals and Catholics Together" have dealt with such theological issues as "The Gift of Salvation" (1997), "The Communion of Saints" (2003), "The Call to Holiness" (2005), and "Do Whatever He Tells You: The Blessed Virgin Mary in Christian Faith and Life" (2009).

In both cases, Evangelical and Fundamentalist reaction included both positive and negative responses to the dialogue. That is to be expected. After all, Evangelicals do find many Catholic doctrines and practices untenable. More to the point, however, is the fact that dialogue and conversation did take place and that Catholics and some Evangelicals are able to affirm a common Christian witness. Indeed, this makes for a new situation between the two traditions, especially since an anti-Catholic polemic often informed past (and many present!) Fundamentalist and Evangelical positions. Also, the fact that Catholic ecumenism now extends to Evangelicals as it does to mainline Protestants is significant as well.

Finally, one sector of Evangelicalism that has not received attention thus far but has conducted an even more sustained dialogue with the Catholic Church is Pentecostalism. Familiar to Catholics in their own communion as the "charismatic renewal," Pentecostalism is that branch of Evangelicalism that emphasizes the power and gifts of the Holy Spirit in the life of the believer and the church. Usually the Christian is exhorted to seek "Baptism in the Holy Spirit," a spiritual experience of empowerment that is evidenced by the gifts of the Spirit. *Glossolalia* or "speaking in tongues" is considered by many Pentecostals as the premier sign or even "initial evidence" that one has received Spirit-baptism. Because of the discerning acceptance of the charismatic renewal in the Catholic Church, the Pontifical Council for Promoting Christian Unity in Rome and its Pentecostal dialogue partners have produced five final reports from 1972 to 2006 as a result of their conversations. This dialogue is a good example of how the Evangelical emphasis on Christian experience and piety (what Catholics often call spirituality) can be a constructive tool and model for ecumenical conversation. Pentecostalism in particular directs attention to this issue even more so than other Evangelical movements whose primary concern is with the authority of Scripture. Although this dialogue is quite substantial theologically speaking, it has yet to gain acceptance among some Pentecostal leaders who oppose ecumenism, or among the many independent Pentecostal congregations where the level of theological literacy is not high, including that of many of their pastors. Nevertheless, it is one of the most promising of ecumenical dialogues taking place.

PART II

Points of Understanding between Catholic and Evangelical Christians

ONE
Overcoming Stereotypes

We begin by identifying some common stereotypes that members of one tradition sometimes have of the other. It is best to overcome these as soon as possible, even if there is some truth to them, as is the case with most stereotypes. Not only are we required to get beyond these stereotypes by Christian charity, but also by the sincere pursuit of truth to which Christ calls us.

Common Evangelical Attitudes toward Catholics

Two of the most common attitudes that Evangelical Christians have toward Catholics are that the structures and rites of the church hinder us from having a personal relationship with Jesus Christ and that salvation is accomplished through our own efforts, that is, through our good works. While they admit there have been genuine Christians in the Catholic Church, especially among our saints and mystics, it seems to them that the average Catholic simply goes through various rituals and just tries to be a good person. However, when it comes to knowing the reality of Jesus Christ and sharing his good news with others, Catholics seem to fall far short. For the most part many Catholics seem to be just nominal Christians.

To get beyond these stereotypes we shall return to the Evangelical dimension of Catholic church life and sacramentality and to the Catholic understanding of grace. For the moment it might benefit Catholics to consider how many of those who have been sacramentally initiated into the Catholic Church through baptism, confirmation, and Eucharist are in the need of profound evangelization. Interestingly enough, when Catholics do share their faith, as many charismatic Catholics do, Evangelicals are quick to recognize them as true "born again" Christians!

Common Catholic Attitudes toward Evangelicals

On the other side, it is difficult for many Catholics to get beyond their first contact impression of Evangelical Christians. They are sure of their salvation. Is this a matter of Evangelical pride and self-righteousness or something else? They quote the Bible a lot. But is it in context and have they made of it some sort of law that is even more severe than that of the

Catholic Church? This may be especially true, for example, for those Catholics with an abundance of pre–Vatican II memories. Also, the Evangelical emphasis on a personal relationship with Christ seems to exclude a social and communal dimension to faith. But, on the other hand, they have very active congregational lives as compared to many Catholic parishes.

Some contemporary Catholics who consider themselves progressive and liberal wonder if Evangelicals' high view of biblical authority is simply a quest for certainty and security in an authority that is analogous to conservative Catholics who rigorously adhere to the pronouncements of the papal and episcopal magisterium, the teaching office of the church. Some conservative Catholics wonder if Evangelical Christians envision no authority higher than their own private judgment in the interpretation of Scripture. Are they fitting the Word of God then to their own needs and convictions? And what about the unity of the church? Are there not more Evangelical groups and denominations than any other kind? If they truly abide by the Word of God why are there so many divisions among them? Many of these impressions ring true. Do they take biblical scholarship seriously and what do they mean when they profess their spiritual unity in Christ but remain in separate denominational and parachurch structures?

Two
What We Share in Common

More than is realized by most Christians, whether Evangelical or Catholic, the two traditions have much in common. At the very least they may recognize each other as fellow Christians and followers of Christ. A more hopeful scenario envisions their witness as a common one although doctrinal differences still prevent some forms of cooperation. The important point at this stage is the realization that common witness is possible even if structural unity is not. Moreover, Christian ecumenical dialogue requires ongoing conversion and the theological virtues of faith, hope, and love.

Not all Evangelicals are interested in dialogue. Even some Catholics still view relations with Protestants solely as an opportunity for their conversion to Catholicism. Our intent is to apply the consistent teaching on ecumenism that the church has articulated since the Second Vatican Council. We begin with three areas of core Christian beliefs that Evangelicals and Catholics hold in common.

Reverence for Scripture

Sacred Scripture is at the heart of the Christian witness to divine revelation. The Evangelical commitment to biblical truth and study is impressive and commendable. However, this is no less true for Catholic and Orthodox believers as it is for Protestants. Granted, Scripture and tradition together transmit divine revelation for Catholics and Orthodox, while Protestants hold to *sola scriptura* (Scripture alone) as the revelatory norm. We shall touch upon these differences in the next section. Nevertheless, the impact of the Bible on Catholic life is as great as it is for Evangelical Protestants. A few examples illustrate this.

The reading of Scripture pervades the liturgical life of Catholics. The Liturgy of the Word during Mass consists of the proclamation of the Word from Scripture with probably more portions of the Bible being read during worship than at your average Evangelical Sunday worship service (for example, three readings and a psalm versus sometimes one reading from which the minister will preach). The official public prayer of the church in the Liturgy of the Hours (Office of Readings, Morning Prayer, Evening Prayer) revolves around the psalter (all 150 psalms are recited during a four-week cycle) and biblical readings (one long one for the Office; short ones for the Prayers), with additional biblical canticles and prayers based upon Scripture passages. The tradition of contemplative and meditative prayer for personal communion with God has long made use of *lectio divina* (divine reading) from the monastic tradition. This prayerful reading of Scripture has inspired many Catholic Christians—religious, clerical, and lay—to live in God's presence and to heed the call to discipleship and the practice of the Christian life.

Another area of church life where the Bible has profound significance is in church teaching itself. Because the Reformation presented the teaching of Scripture over against the teaching of Catholic tradition and church authority, and the lay reading of Scripture and Bible study was not as pervasive among Catholics as among Protestants, it was sometimes thought that the Bible had little to do with church doctrine and theology. Not true. The church fathers and scholastic doctors often wrote commentaries on Scripture and even the Counter-Reformation Council of Trent (1545–63) made appeal to the Bible. However, it is clearly the case that Catholic biblical study was renewed during the pontificate of Pius XII with the promulgation of his encyclical *Divino Afflante Spiritu* (1943) and under the influence of the Second Vatican Council (1962–65) Scripture has ever more deeply informed various levels of church teaching. More to the point, the Catholic Church, whether at prayer or in the proclamation and instruction of the faith, is steeped in the biblical word.

Catholics who encounter Evangelicals and are impressed with how familiar they are with the Bible need to realize how much the Bible is already a part of Catholic life. Reading the Scripture with Evangelicals will certainly highlight differences of interpretation. Not all issues will be resolved. But if there is to be a common witness, Catholics would do well to retrieve their biblical roots and be nurtured even more by the Bible as the written Word of God. Furthermore, as we shall see, Catholic doctrine can be expressed in biblical language. This will help Evangelicals understand and appreciate Catholicism. Also, Evangelicals hold to many central Christian beliefs such as the Trinity and the incarnation.

During the formulation of these core dogmas nonbiblical language was often used in order to express the truth of these beliefs. The spread and success of the faith into new cultures such as the Greco-Roman world of antiquity necessitated this in order to be faithful to the truth as originally held. In today's theological language the faith needed to be inculturated into the language and thought forms of other cultures. This is never a one-way street, for it often transforms culture in the process. Evangelicals are beginning to recognize this as they realize that their central doctrines were formulated during the great period of the Latin and Greek church fathers in the first seven centuries after Christ. By the second century what we now know as the Catholic structure of the church was already operative, so Evangelicals simply cannot dismiss this period as a postbiblical falling away from the truth of the apostolic church.

The Centrality of Christ

One of the fundamentals to which Evangelicals are still committed is the divinity of Christ. Evangelical believers are Christ-centered to the extent that the uniqueness of Christ is a common Evangelical theme. He is the only way to the Father, and a personal relationship with Christ as Savior and Lord beats at the heart of Evangelical piety and spirituality. The sinner who comes to Christ for salvation and the "born-again" believer who loves Jesus and wants to be faithful to him in all areas of life both personify the Evangelical Christian. With its roots in pietism and revivalism, these seem to the Evangelical to be the only true manifestations of Christian piety. How can anyone claim to be a Christian and not be devoted to Christ, have faith in Christ for salvation, and be stirred in the depths of one's heart by the Savior's love for us? To outsiders this could seem exclusive and tinged with not a little bit of religious sentimentality.

Are Catholics any less devoted to Christ? Does their devotion to Mary and the saints obscure the centrality of Christ? Are they so ritually bound that the heartfelt love for Jesus gets buried beneath external observances? These are the types of questions an Evangelical is interested in, although even to some mainstream liberal Protestants, Evangelical piety and doctrine are as foreign as they are to Catholics. But it is not untypical for a Catholic to feel deeply challenged by the testimony of Evangelicals. With the exception of many charismatics, most Catholics are not used to speaking of the affective (that is, the more emotion-based) dimension of their faith. What is an experience of God like? When asked by an Evangelical whether one knows Christ, they might answer that surely they believe in Christ. But then the question returns: But do you really know him? Something more is being asked than the mere affirmation of certain beliefs.

The answer to all these questions is a strong "yes," but at many different levels. There is no more Christ-centered event than the Catholic celebration of the Eucharist, which takes place within a Trinitarian framework (more about this later). Even as Catholics deeply reverence Scripture, they also cherish the true reality and presence of Christ. What could be more Christ-centered than the sacramental presence of Christ in the eucharistic elements: in his body and blood, soul and divinity? Vatican II's Constitution on the Sacred Liturgy came to express Christ's presence and action throughout the life of the church: in the persons of his ministers, in his Word when the Holy Scriptures are read, when the church prays and sings, and in the spiritual and apostolic life of the faithful. The point is that the Catholic understanding of Christian and church life is simply the reality of Jesus

Christ present and active among his people, and it is this that constitutes the church as his Body.

If it is the case that the public liturgy of the church thus presents the reality of Jesus Christ in the fullness of his saving action, it is also true that the eucharistic focus of this action is his paschal mystery, that is, his saving death and resurrection. Evangelicals have a difficult time with the Catholic Eucharist. They envision it as another human work by which the Catholic Church attempts to gain righteousness by offering Christ as an unbloody sacrifice to the Father. But Evangelicals misread Catholic truth. In fact, Catholics are closer to Evangelicals than it might appear on this matter. And again, it all has to do with the centrality of Christ. Evangelicals will often speak of the "finished work" of Christ. Quoting the New Testament that Christ died once and for all (Rom 6:10; Heb 7:27), they perceive the Catholic affirmation of the eucharistic sacrifice as something additional to his salvific work on Calvary, as if the latter was not complete or sufficient. In their view this diminishes Christ's sacrifice on the cross. But, in fact, it is precisely because of its all-sufficiency that Catholics understand the Eucharist to be a re-presentation of Christ's offering on the cross. If Christ is really present in the Eucharist, then he is present as the Lamb of God, as the one who offers himself on our behalf. Our offering of Christ is simply entering into his offering before the Father. Through the Eucharist, Catholics enter into the depths of Christ.

For both Evangelicals and Catholics Christ is absolutely central. It would be unrealistic to expect Evangelicals to accept a Catholic theology of the Eucharist. But it is not unreasonable to witness to the Eucharist on terms that an Evangelical can understand for very Evangelical reasons, namely, that the Gospel message is to communicate Christ as Savior. Nor is Catholic devotion to Christ limited to the Eucharist. The affective awareness of Christ's saving presence is reflected in many of the sacramentals of the church, of which paraliturgical devotions are a part, for example, devotion to the Sacred Heart. The mystical and spiritual traditions of the church also witness to this. Who could question the love for Christ manifested in St. Francis of Assisi or embedded in the *Spiritual Exercises* of St. Ignatius Loyola, the founder of the Society of Jesus (the Jesuits)? Evangelicals and Catholics may not doctrinally agree on the specifics of how Christ is central to Christian faith, but the mutual recognition that he is central in both traditions opens the door to dialogue and spiritual fellowship between them.

The Call to Mission

Without a doubt British and American Evangelicals were at the forefront of Protestant missionary efforts during the nineteenth century. This has left an indelible mark on Evangelicalism and still informs its followers' sense of Christian identity and obligation.

Whether through foreign or home missions, Evangelicals have been strong supporters of these efforts. Parachurch missionary and evangelistic organizations abound in addition to denominational mission boards and local church missionaries. The former may be interdenominational in the cooperation they elicit or may be purely independent of ecclesiastical structures. What counts is that the witness to Christ in the highways and byways of the world abounds with the expectation that many will hear, believe, and convert to Jesus Christ as Lord and Savior.

Catholics are no strangers to mission and the missionary enterprise. Not only did Catholic missionary efforts keep up with those of Protestants in the last century, they preceded Protestant missions for a good two centuries, if not more. While the newly formed Protestant churches were consolidating their gains and identity in the sixteenth and seventeenth centuries, Catholic missionaries were spreading the Gospel both during and immediately after the Reformation. One need only recall the journeys of St. Francis Xavier (d. 1552) to south and east Asia, not to mention the vast missionary efforts by monks during late antiquity and into the early Middle Ages. Missionary congregations still exist (the Maryknollers in the United States are a good example), and many Catholics still remember and still experience the visits of missioners to their local parish as well as the "parish mission" itself, a form of home missionary outreach.

The real issue, however, is not who can best the other in missionary work, but what do we mean by mission and how does it form our ecclesial identity?

It is no coincidence that the first official international dialogue between Roman Catholics and Evangelicals focused on mission. The dialogue known by the acronym ERCDOM (Evangelical–Roman Catholic Dialogue on Mission) in 1984 identified both convergences and differences in their respective commitments to mission. Among the commonalities were convictions about the foundational Christian doctrines of creation, revelation, salvation, and judgment. For example, in reference to the creative love of God, both sides acknowledge God's revelatory gift in human history and in the truth present in other religious traditions, either through general revelation (Evangelical term) or the work of the Logos (Catholic emphasis). Both acknowledge by virtue of the free initiative of God's grace that Christ is the only Savior and that the church is subject to judgment if it is not faithful to the Gospel mandate to proclaim the good news of salvation.

Despite differences between their two traditions, Evangelicals and Catholics posit the call to mission as integral to Christian and ecclesial life. Mission means more than just missionary efforts; it is at the core of what it means to be "church." Certainly Catholics emphasize the ecclesial dimension much more. It is the church that is in mission. Evangelicals are more flexible when it comes to church bodies and structures, although they are rather firm in their congregational commitments. The key for them is that mission is being carried out one way or the other.

A review of the documents of the Second Vatican Council reveals that mission is one of the most formative ecclesial themes. The Decree on the Church's Missionary Activity *(Ad gentes divinitus)*, the Dogmatic Constitution on the Church *(Lumen Gentium)*, and the Pastoral Constitution on the Church in the Modern World *(Gaudium et Spes)* are all permeated by this sensibility of the church existing in mission. The redemptive missions of the Son and the Holy Spirit constitute the church as the people of God, the body of Christ, and the temple of the Holy Spirit. By participating in the life of the triune God, mission becomes the dynamic of the human journey from creation to fulfillment in the kingdom of God. And, as we will see in our examination of some of the differences between the two traditions, this sense of mission has enhanced our appreciation of evangelization and witness. For the Catholic Christian in dialogue with our Evangelical brothers and sisters, the realization of the full scope of mission and of its permanent orientation to the Gospel of Jesus Christ is key.

THREE

Some Differences

The Relationship between the Authority of Scripture and the Authority of the Church (and Tradition)

We have already seen hints of differences within a basic commonality shared by Catholics and Evangelicals. The ERCDOM statement identified revelation as one of those commonalities. However, even a glance at how each understands the process and authority of divine revelation exposes some significant differences, many of which go back directly to the Reformation itself. Specifically, what is the role of tradition in revelation and what authority does it bear in relation to Sacred Scripture?

Among all Protestants, Evangelicals are probably the most adamant in preserving the Reformation principle of *sola scriptura*: Scripture alone as the divinely mandated authority for Christian faith and practice.

Revelation is primarily mediated to the church through the written word of God in Scripture. There, Jesus Christ, the incarnate Word of God, is revealed, and it is from Scripture that the preached word derives its authority. General revelation (as distinct from the special revelation of Scripture) in nature, human experience, and history can only be interpreted in light of biblical truth and cannot contradict it.

There are two main issues that Evangelicals will press in their dialogue with Catholics on this matter. First, they will object to the Catholic belief that tradition conveys revelation along with Scripture. Second, they will call into question the authority of the church to define and teach Christian doctrine and therefore to interpret Scripture. Both tradition and the church's teaching office in their view compromise the authority of the Bible. In this respect Catholics are subject to human error in their doctrine and have acquired a number of church beliefs and practices that from the Evangelical's perspective have no precedent in the Bible. It is precisely here that the Catholic claim that the church as divinely authorized by Christ is called into question. In fact, it seems in many areas that the only authority for some beliefs and practices is simply the human (and therefore very fallible!) authority of church leaders. How to respond?

Again, in dialogue we are not attempting to persuade Evangelicals to accept the Catholic position on these matters. Rather we are attempting to explain them in such a way that reinforces what Evangelicals accept as the primary message of the Gospel, namely, Jesus Christ offered for the salvation of the world. It makes more sense to explain why Catholics understand that tradition transmits revelation along with Scripture and that this does not contradict or call into question the authority of the Bible. In fact, demonstrating that the Word of God is effective in the life of the church by being present in its tradition reinforces the authority of Scripture. Then one may turn to specific Catholic doctrines, which Evangelicals are wont to consider nonbiblical, for example, the Marian dogmas, the sacrament of reconciliation or confession, purgatory, etcetera, and defend their evangelical integrity and the fact that they bear witness to the saving truth of the Gospel.

One may argue that the Catholic approach to revelation takes account of both the process of revelation and its fruits. While Catholics bear witness to the integrity and authority of Scripture and its place in church teaching and practice, they also look to the very Christian community out of which Scripture as the Word of God arose. It was this early Christian community that, through meditation on the Scriptures, produced many elemental teachings that even Evangelicals accept. However, to use the chicken-and-egg analogy, the church as a community of believers existed *before* the canon of the New Testament was either written or recognized, and it was from within the life of the church that the Gospels and Epistles of the New Testament were written and then collected into an authoritative canon. To be sure, the church never understood itself as being above the Word of God, but always as its servant, as the Second Vatican Council's Dogmatic Constitution on Divine Revelation *(Dei Verbum)* was to articulate in no uncertain terms.

To suggest however that it is a matter of chronology only is really to do a disservice to the church's grasp of revelation. That example only serves to highlight that the Word of God comes to us through the integrated process by which Sacred Scripture, sacred tradition, and the teaching authority or magisterium of the church came into being. The divine Word as God's revelation permeates all aspects of the church's life, with priority given to the apostolic preaching and its transmission through the written word of Scripture and through tradition. This constitutes the "Sacred deposit" of the faith "entrusted to the whole of the Church" with "the living teaching office of the Church alone," the successors of the apostles, exercising responsibility to authentically interpret the Word of God *(Catechism of the Catholic Church*, nos. 84, 85).

Evangelicals will most likely not accept this presentation of the issues, for they will be wary of the role of tradition as compared to the Bible. But it will be helpful to clarify that the Catholic rejection of the Protestant principle of *sola scriptura* is due to a profound appreciation of the incarnational dimension of

God's Word in its entire saving and truth-bearing efficacy. Catholics attempt to reverence and obey this Word by enfleshing it and acknowledging its presence in the life of the church as the body of Christ. This is a far cry from the misconception that by tradition we are simply compromising or reducing it to mere human custom.

The Different Languages of Conversion

If there is a distinguishing mark of Evangelicalism that is lodged in both the popular mind as well as in its own self-understanding, it is the call of conversion to Jesus Christ. Typically, an Evangelical Christian is able to identify the day when he or she was converted. Different terms may be used to describe or label the experience, and an experience it usually is. One may speak of accepting Jesus Christ as one's personal Lord and Savior, or of receiving Christ into one's life. Many use the language of "being born again," which corresponds to the Christian doctrine of regeneration, which we will address shortly. The experience may have a strong affective quality to it, but even if it does not, one can still rely on the divine promise that one's sins are forgiven by the acknowledgment of Christ as one's own Savior. John Wesley, the founder of Methodism, expressed it best, as we have seen, when he described his own experience in terms of his heart being strangely warmed. The key is the sense of "assurance" that God loves me and has accepted me in Christ.

Of course, there are variations of this theme in Evangelicalism, with some placing more emphasis on the affective dimension (the emotional tone of the conversion), and some emphasizing more the volitional dimension (the decision to personally accept Christ). So while the majority of Evangelicals endorse a "believer's baptism" only, there are others who still practice infant baptism. All of them agree, however, that at some point the baptized person needs to *personally* appropriate the Gospel for him- or herself. Baptism or church membership will not save you! Only Christ saves. So accept him into your heart! That's the message.

The famous Harvard psychologist of religion, William James, in his classic book, *The Varieties of Religious Experience*, once described this sort of experience as the "twice-born," as contrasted with the "once-born" type of religious person. It would be too simplistic to describe Evangelicals as "twice-born" Christians and Catholics as "once-born" Christians, but there is some truth to the observation. Another way of describing one's basic religiosity is the difference between those for whom their faith has been a gradual development in life and those for whom it was founded on a crisis experience of faith. Again, Evangelicals and Catholics can be found in both camps, but it does seem as if the classic Evangelical conversion usually emerges out of some sense of sin in one's life that is now forgiven through faith in the Savior. It is characterized and often feels like a rebirth in one's inner life and worldview. How can Catholic Christians make sense of this type of testimony among their Evangelical brothers and sisters?

For one thing, crisis conversions are not unknown in the Catholic tradition. The most famous case was that of St. Augustine. Although the process of conversion took years of searching on his part, he certainly could remember the day, when upon hearing the voice of a child, his heart was settled by the peace of Christ. Other saints had similar experiences, often turning very radically from a life of sin or indifference to a wholehearted following of Christ. Catholics should remember and celebrate such testimonies, as indeed we do every year on January 25th, the feast of the conversion of St. Paul the Apostle.

For most Catholics, however, especially the majority who were baptized as infants, such crisis experiences are not that common. This does not rule out a renewed sense of faith that many undergo at some point in their lives. Through the instrumentality of a retreat, movements such as Cursillo or the Charismatic renewal, or maybe just a gradual realization and desire, some people become more active in their faith, prayer, and service. Is this conversion in the Evangelical sense? Yes and no!

The crisis conversions described above are similar

to the Evangelical idea of conversion. A strong sense of sin and grace is often present, and the overwhelming sense of God's mercy in the good news of Jesus Christ can attend the event. Experiences of renewal can be very dramatic and affective in tone or very quiet and only moderately emotional. In both cases conversion is operative in a person's life. For baptized Catholics the language of conversion is used for those who newly enter the church. Many theologians, however, have come to use the language of conversion to describe how different aspects of one's life, (e.g., the intellectual, the moral, the religious) may mature, or how our lives are involved in a continuous process of conversion as we grow in grace and in the theological virtues of faith, hope, and love.

So Christian conversion as understood by Catholics has to do mainly with the continual ongoing transformation of the human person into the image of Christ. Indeed there is an initial dimension to the conversion process as represented in parish RCIA programs (Rite of Christian Initiation of Adults). Even in this case there is a major difference with the prevailing practices within Evangelicalism. Those entering the church engage in a lengthy process of conversion (at the very least for several months) in which they are prepared to receive the converting sacraments of initiation (Baptism, Confirmation, Eucharist). Anybody engaged in RCIA knows the rewards of this process. The sensibility and wisdom operative here have to do with the profound respect the church has for the process of conversion of life and for the dignity of every human person. By contrast, Evangelicals will consider one converted if a decision is made for Christ at an evangelistic crusade. To be sure, the Evangelical ideal is that the new "born again" Christian will join a local church and engage in the Christian disciplines that promote discipleship and sanctification: regular worship, Bible study, prayer, witness, and service. But the sensibility is different, and for this we turn to some important theological issues.

For Evangelicals, conversion entails a before and after, not only psychologically for the person, but theologically as well. The classic hymn "Amazing Grace" expresses it well: "I once was lost but now am found, was blind but now I see."

The reception of grace—what Evangelicals refer to as being saved or being "born again"—marks the death of the old person in Adam and the rebirth of the new person in Christ. Believer's baptism by immersion as practiced by many Evangelicals effectively symbolizes this. For Evangelicals, the only forms of grace operative before conversion might be "prevenient grace" or "common grace." Prevenient grace is that which leads to conversion, and in the Wesleyan tradition, it refers to the grace by which God moves the sinner's heart to desire God. Common grace enables moral capacity, and in the Reformed tradition this means that non-Christians receive grace to act morally in civil society even though this is not saving grace to know Jesus

Christ. However, the notion that grace is active through sacramental reception (such as in infant baptism) is absent from Evangelicalism, except for those who are in the more sacramental traditions, such as Evangelical Anglicans.

So a Catholic believes that God's grace is present and active in a person's life *even before an experience of spiritual renewal*, while an Evangelical, in contrast, is quite content to acknowledge that before grace came one was dead in sin, and while God may have been at work before that, it was only to lead a person to conversion. Only people spiritually dead in sin can be born again. Catholics, who are regenerated through the grace given in baptism, are not born again through a postbaptismal conversion experience but are renewed in their sacramental faith. Therefore, Catholics pastorally gear people to the process of conversion (initial and ongoing) while Evangelicals are focused on leading a person to Christ for the first time. Catholics can agree that God works in both ways, even if they differ with Evangelicals about the theology of conversion.

What should a Catholic say when asked if he or she is born again? Stick with the faith of the church. We were born again in baptism. God's grace is at work even before our readiness to accept it. It is all gift! Evangelicals will like that language (grace, after all, is free!) even if they do not accept our Catholic faith and practice. Dialogue will then begin with our common testimony to the gift of God in Christ. The authenticity of our practice will bear witness to the truth of our faith (Christ's grace in the sacraments) as the fruit of conversion is evident in our lives.

The Role of Experience

Experience is a loaded word. What do we mean by it and what are its characteristics? Religious experience in particular is the subject of much investigation and analysis. What does it mean to experience God? Evangelicals on the whole seem to be fairly big on experience, especially in the form of testimony to how Christ saved them or how he is working in their lives. As already observed, different types of Evangelicals will have diverse opinions on the role and importance of religious experience. Pentecostals will certainly emphasize it more than, for example, Evangelicals of a Fundamentalist bent, or those who are strongly influenced by the Reformed tradition in theology and who want to stress that faith in God's Word is much more important than experience. Experience can be variable, while God's Word is always stable and sure.

Catholics for the most part are more cautious about religious experience, although they have a long and venerated history of spiritual discernment that attempts to evaluate the experiences one has in prayer and the overall direction of one's life in the Spirit. Associated with this is the clear acknowledgment of the mystical tradition in the history of the church along with the recognition that many of the saints were quite gifted with experiences of the divine presence. These are attributed to the infusion of God's grace with the understanding that God is free to distribute such mystical graces to whomever God wills.

At the level of popular piety or "devotional Catholicism," emotion and desire often play a significant role for those who practice the various devotions to Jesus, Mary, and the saints. In more recent years, the spread of the Charismatic renewal in the Catholic Church has nourished experiences of the presence of Christ that are not that dissimilar to those witnessed to in Evangelical testimonies. In light of this, however, it would not be an overstatement to suggest that the level of religious experience in your average Evangelical congregation is probably higher than in your average Catholic parish. In part this is due to the "free-church" nature of many Evangelical communities. Evangelicals actively select their particular church communities on the basis of the high value that these churches place on conversion, as described in our previous section. In contrast, Catholic parishes simply cover all the Catholics in a geographical area, and Catholics tend to worship in the church that is located in the area where they live. But there are theological reasons as well.

While it is true that there has been a long and sustained tradition of spiritual direction (or guidance) and discernment in Catholicism, there has also been a theological tradition of reserve and caution when it comes to religious experience. New movements of renewal and new charisms mediated by saints were met not only with caution, but sometimes with resistance by church authorities. Many times the recognition of a new charism or gift took place at the grass-roots level long before being recognized by the pastoral office of the church. In part this comes with the territory. A pastor must be concerned about the safety of his flock before allowing it to be led into new pastures. But there is also a theological conundrum that reinforces this pastoral caution. I will state it as a question: How can Catholics affirm a new movement of grace when we are not certain that we are even in a state of grace? This is worth some attention especially in contrast to an Evangelical perspective on this issue.

A significant stream of Catholic theology, at least since the Council of Trent (1545–63), the Counter-Reformation council, expressed great reservations about equating religious experience in the absolute sense with the operation of God's grace in one's life. There was concern on the part of the Catholic Church about the problem of "religious enthusiasm," or excessive and unorthodox spiritual practices. The question that arose in light of the Protestant Reformation was whether one could be assured of one's personal salvation, which for a Catholic meant that one claimed that one was in a state of grace, specifically, sanctifying or habitual grace. As the council stated: "No one can know with the certainty of faith, in such a way as to exclude the possibility of error, that he has obtained the grace of God" (Decree on Justification, chapter ix). Remember, Catholics pray at the end of the Hail Mary: "...pray for us sinners now and at the hour of our death." The certainty of one's personal salvation (requiring the presence of grace) is not a given. This does not exclude awareness of how God is touching one's life, however. We can be aware of sanctifying or habitual grace, which makes us holy, as well as actual grace, which helps us with specific needs or in a particular circumstance, or simply to grow in the holiness that God has already imparted.

But with the warning expressed by the Council of Trent, some theologians went so far as to suggest that one could not be certain whether any so-called religious experience was a consequence of God's grace or not. That being the case then, many priests schooled in such theology were not enthusiastic about claims to religious experience among those subject to their pastoral care or spiritual direction.

Contrast this with your typical Evangelical Christian. They stress to an even greater degree than the Reformers themselves (Martin Luther and John Calvin) that the assurance of salvation is a matter of personal experience. The Spirit indeed witnesses to people that the divine promise of salvation in Jesus Christ has become a reality in their lives, and therefore they can be certain of their home in heaven. This is even more the case in congregations with a revivalist ethos, where believers expect that in the realm of experience the promise and assurance of salvation will become a matter of subjective and existential reality. The "heart-work" of religion is the norm, not the exception.

Where do we go from here? There are several factors that one must consider. First, the theological caution about religious experience that we reviewed is no longer dominant in Catholic theological circles. Second, even as we still hold to the definition of the Council of Trent, we also must consider the venerated history of mysticism and spiritual discernment in various Catholic spiritualities. Therefore, we might venture the following: Catholics are not as reticent in the area of religious experience as was once the case. Nevertheless, we are more focused on the motions of grace than we are regarding the state of grace. We tend to ask how we are cooperating with the movement of grace in our lives rather than concentrating on whether or not we are in a state of grace. The former is not unrelated to the latter, however. To grow in grace is to nurture and develop all those virtues and habits that enhance and sustain the Christian life, including cooperating with actual graces and the gifts and charisms of the Holy Spirit. To Evangelicals, this sounds more like sanctification than justification. But more on this below. What will be helpful for Evangelicals is to hear from Catholics that the saving presence of Christ is a reality in their lives and that what transpires in the sacraments is not just external ritual but is fully integrated with a life of Christian discipline, service, and prayer.

Evangelization and Evangelism!

Evangelization and evangelism. Are they different or just two ways of saying the same thing, namely to witness to the good news of Jesus Christ? Catholics do tend to use the former and Evangelicals the latter term. Evangelization does, however, have broader connotations than evangelism. All forms of witness to Christ are included, not just personal witness and public preaching of the Gospel in an explicitly evangelistic message for the unconverted.

To be fair, both Catholic and Evangelicals utilize the two terms. In fact it was in the mid-seventies that both traditions reconsidered the importance of evangelization. In 1974 the International Congress on World Evangelization was held in Lausanne, Switzerland, the result of which was the proclamation of "The Lausanne Covenant," an agreed statement on evangelism and mission by this international representation of the world's Evangelicals. The covenant defines evangelism as "the proclamation of the historical, biblical Christ as Saviour and Lord, with a view to persuading people to come to him personally and so be reconciled to God." It also mentioned "obedience to Christ, incorporation into his Church and responsible service in the world" as consequences of evangelism, with a clear understanding that this includes Christian social responsibility and activity as an accompaniment of and bridge to the preaching of the Gospel (as a later Lausanne report articulated in 1982).

For Catholics 1975 marked a similar concentration on the subject when Pope Paul VI promulgated his Apostolic Exhortation (*Evangelii Nuntiandi*, "On Evangelization in the Modern World"). Regarding the relationship between evangelization and human advancement and liberation, it posits a similar connection as articulated in the Lausanne Covenant. While evangelization cannot be reduced to social advancement, it cannot be disassociated from it either. As the Dialogue on Mission states, both would agree that "Social responsibility is an integral part of evangelization; and the struggle for justice can be a manifestation of the kingdom of God." There is more agreement than many Evangelicals and Catholics would suspect. At the more popular level the differences are sharper.

Most Evangelicals emphasize preaching and witness to win people to Christ. Church membership and Christian service follow from this. Catholics, on the other hand, tend to focus on evangelization as part of an overall church mission that envisions all ministries as part and parcel of its task to spread the good news. That people are drawn to Christ happens within the context of their entry into the church and, it is presumed, in their preparation to receive the sacraments of initiation. Catholic parishes or renewal movements may indeed engage in openly evangelistic activities, usually directed at nominal Catholics, many of whom are already baptized. While Catholics sometimes try to evangelize the "unchurched," their efforts in this area usually don't match the energy of Evangelicals. Why is this?

First, Catholics more than Evangelicals affirm the possibility of salvation for non-Christians and for all people of good will. Many Evangelicals would deny this possibility; hence, their concern to save souls. Catholics also tend to stress witnessing the Gospel by living an exemplary Christian life more than by preaching, although Paul VI (and John Paul II following him) considered the verbal proclamation of the Gospel message indispensable. Evangelicals do not discount the importance of living according to the Gospel as a form of witnessing the faith, but they do stress that every Christian can verbally witness, even if it is only through the sharing of how one came to Christ.

Second, the Catholic Church considers interreligious dialogue—that is, dialogue between Christians and members of non-Christian religious traditions—to be integral to evangelization. Such dialogues are not intended to gain converts, but they are also not intended to mute the message of the Gospel. Some Evangelicals are engaged in similar dialogues, but many do not believe non-Christian traditions can be vehicles of salvation. Catholics would agree that non-Christian religions are not equivalent or complementary means of salvation or revelation. However, while Catholics still maintain that Christ and the church are the ordinary means of salvation, they also acknowledge that Christ, through his Spirit, can save people apart from these means. To what extent this happens with members of non-Christian traditions remains an open theological question, since the Catholic Church rejects nothing that is true and holy in them, while simultaneously maintaining the unicity and salvific universality of Jesus Christ and the church (see *Dominus Iesus*, promulgated by the Congregation for the Doctrine of the Faith in 2000).

In sum, the Evangelical theology of mission and evangelization presses its adherents to seek converts as the main point of evangelism. Catholics envision a whole range of activity as witnessing to the Gospel, including the evangelization of culture and society. Explicit proclamation to the unconverted and to non-practicing Catholics is not excluded; it is even encouraged and promoted by the church. Confident in the hope of God's mercy to all, Catholics usually do not seek out the lost (as understood by Evangelicals!) with the fervency of their Evangelical brothers and sisters. Here both traditions can learn from each other. As a vocation proper to the church, Paul VI stressed that indeed the church is an evangelizer and an evangelizing community, "but she begins by being evangelized herself" *(Evangelii Nuntiandi)*.

FOUR

What Every Catholic Should Be Aware of When Relating to Evangelicals

The following comments attempt to summarize some key points that arise between Catholics and Evangelicals. While we have covered some of this ground already, here we present it more briefly, and yet with some additional points, in order to locate our differences within a framework that emphasizes our commonality in the faith of Jesus Christ.

Salvation as an Evangelical's Experience/Crisis/Decision, and Salvation as a Catholic's Process

Salvation is the focus of Evangelical faith, and the experience of it is a given for Evangelical fellowship. Jesus Christ once for all accomplished salvation on the cross for the whole world and this can become a matter of personal experience. One can encounter Jesus Christ as personal Lord and Savior, meaning that in prayer one has an encounter with Christ in which sin is acknowledged and repented and Christ is received in faith as the only one who can save one from the penalty and consequences of sin. While the emotive or affective tonality of the experience may vary, there is a "before and after" to conversion that entails a critical break with one's past life. Even for those raised in Evangelical families and churches the possibilities of a crisis experience exist, though it may be quite subdued. Most importantly, one decides (with God's grace!) to accept Christ. It is one's personal appropriation of the Gospel that is at the heart of Evangelicalism, with the expectation of life-changing consequences.

Catholics, on the other hand, certainly do not rule out crisis experiences. The lives of many a saint began with such an event. But the theological emphasis that conversion is a daily struggle along with a sacramental understanding of the mediation of grace shifts attention away from a particular event in grace to the process of growing in grace. Graced moments are important and even formative for the person so graced, but they are part of an overall life journey with God. Since Evangelicals seek an assurance of the salvation promised to faith, they often experience it. Catholics do not, but that does not mean they are passive. The absence of a doctrine of assurance for

Catholics does not lead to fear of damnation (as sometimes portrayed by Evangelicals) but to the cultivation of the virtues of faith, hope, and love. Salvation is the atmosphere in which one grows, for it pervades the life of the church (through its sacramental and charismatic graces), and the divine mercy is exceedingly rich even in one's personal life. Rather than offering the possibility of knowing with total certainty that one is saved, the church invites a person to participate in God's abundant salvific graces throughout this pilgrim life. Salvation is cumulative for the Catholic, and the extent of it in any person's life is known only to God.

It would be unfair to suggest that Evangelicals are unconcerned about progress in the Christian life; in fact, quite the opposite. In order to understand how Evangelicals and Catholics differ in their concern for Christian formation and growth we need turn to a crucial difference in theology, namely the doctrine of grace.

Grace as God's Favor (Evangelicals) and Grace as God's Inward Working and Human Cooperation (Catholics)

Evangelicals make a crucial distinction between *justification* and *sanctification*, between being made righteous before God and being made holy. Justification is a matter of "imputed" righteousness—God *declares* us to be righteous for Christ's sake, even though (as Martin Luther consistently taught) this righteousness is external; it is Christ's and not our own. God "applies" Christ's righteousness to us as a free gift. It is through faith alone that we can receive this "declaration" that we are righteous, and it comes externally from Christ, not from anything within us. Good works do nothing to make us righteous. With justification, we have the "status" of being righteous, but we are not actually transformed internally.

Sanctification is a different matter. This is the process by which one actually becomes holy. It is founded upon the free grace of justification, but must not be confused with it. Progress in holiness— Protestants differ on the degree to which one can become holy in this life—is a consequence of justification. Whereas justification applies Christ's righteousness to the believer, sanctification is the believer's becoming actually righteous and holy. The former entails one's acceptance before God for the sake of Jesus Christ; the latter conforms one to Jesus Christ and abounds to the divine glory. So Evangelicals make a clean distinction. First, by justification, we are "legally" declared righteous, even though we have not actually changed internally. Then, by sanctification, we are actually made holy. How does Catholic teaching differ from this?

Catholics identify sanctification with the increase of justification or, to put it the other way around, justification begins with the initiation of sanctification.

In the Catholic view, *a person is actually made just or righteous* in justification, not just "declared" just. *Justification for Catholics is therefore a matter of inner transformation.* From a Protestant perspective Catholics collapse justification into sanctification. Catholics, on the other hand, do not differentiate the two events to the point of total separation. Much of the difference has to do with their divergent understandings of grace.

Evangelicals, following the lead of the Protestant Reformation, primarily interpret grace as God's undeserved favor. God turns to the sinner in justification and works inwardly in the person through regeneration and sanctification—all of this is a matter of God's free and undeserved favor. Justification is God's juridical decree that the sinner is declared righteous by faith alone, not as a result of any good works. It is given through saving knowledge of and trust in God's favor alone. The sinner is "clothed" with Christ's righteousness. Justification is what God does *for us*. Regeneration, which happens with justification and can be a personal "born-again" experience, is what God does *in us*, bringing us to new life in Christ. Sanctification is growth in this new life by being made holy through faith in all aspects of one's being and behavior. It bears fruit in good works, but does not happen because of good works. Justification always remains the basis of ongoing sanctification, although Evangelicals differ on whether faith precedes regeneration or is the consequence of it.

Catholics believe that regeneration takes place through the sacramental grace of baptism. They interpret grace as the infusion of new life in both habitual (sanctifying grace) and transient modes (actual grace). *There is no disjunction between God's favor and the actual inner transformation of the person.* The grace received is actually an inner infusion of divine life that heals one of sin and raises the person to share in the triune life of God. In the Spirit through the Son we become sons and daughters of the Father. Of course, this is based on God's favor but with real effects in the believer. The Council of Trent's Decree on Justification (1547) and the *Catechism of the Catholic Church* (1992) both profess that justification is merited for us by the passion of Christ and is based upon the mercy and justice of God. But—and this merits repeating—what distinguishes the Catholic position is that the person is actually *made* just or righteous in justification, not just *declared* just. Again, justification initiates an inner transformation. In the final analysis, Catholics do attribute justification and sanctification to the grace of God, which is totally gift. This is a concept that Evangelicals can appreciate.

Are we then saying that there is really no difference? Not exactly. In less theologically nuanced language it often appears that Catholics are saved by good works and Evangelical Protestants by faith. Without the nuances just listed this sort of stand-off would be extremely problematic. Evangelicals will reproach Catholics for trying to save themselves by "works-righteousness," as if we could be good enough to pass the muster of divine righteousness. Catholics will insist that Evangelicals think they are getting a "free ride" to heaven without any necessary transformation in their lives. Both are misperceptions, and unfortunately Catholics and Evangelicals have much more in common than they think on this issue without blurring the authentic differences that do exist.

With due discretion about the nature of experience noted in the previous section, we may venture the following: The Evangelical emphasis on the personal appropriation of saving grace and the Catholic insistence on the actual transformation of the person that sanctifying grace effects reveal some common concerns that Evangelicals and Catholics share. Both consider it important that the Gospel has an effectual impact upon the person. Furthermore, both believe that the initiative for the Christian life lies with God. Grace is primary (even and especially for Catholics). Both believe that the human person is engaged in the offer of salvation, either through the Evangelical acceptance of Christ or the Catholic cooperation with the grace that God gives. This is neither a "free ride" for Evangelicals nor "works-righteousness" for Catholics. Rather, the Evangelical acceptance of Christ as Savior opens the door to discipleship of him as Lord, and the Catholic emphasis that God's grace elicits and enables our human cooperation issues in the fruit of good works that mature and crown the grace given. In both cases the Christian life flowers as evidence of God's abundant gifts.

Eternal Salvation as Evangelical Certainty and as Catholic Hope

The fullness of salvation is the eschatological hope for both Evangelicals and Catholics. Both traditions have maintained the hope of the parousia (Christ's second coming) even if some Evangelicals (on the Fundamentalist side) have invested a great deal in a last-days fulfillment of God's prophetic plan. As evidenced in the popularity of Hal Lindsey's book *The Late Great Planet Earth* and Tim LeHaye's and Jerry B. Jenkins's novel series *Left Behind*, the expectation of a pretribulation rapture (to be explained in the next section) still attracts the hearts and minds of many Evangelical Christians. I raise this issue of our common hope so as to properly contextualize the promise of eternal life offered to those who believe in Christ. We have already compared the Evangelical belief in the possibility of having absolute assurance of salvation and the traditional Catholic teaching against this idea. Whereas Evangelical assurance frees a person from anxiety about the future state of his or her soul (salvation is totally gift), Catholic hope invites the perpetual engagement of all of one's faculties in the growth of a faith that is formed and sustained by charity (salvation as the fruit of the gifts given by God).

Evangelicals will still maintain belief in the interior witness of the Spirit as the assurance of salvation. The *Catechism of the Catholic Church* still teaches that we cannot "rely on our own feelings or our works to conclude that we are justified and saved." But "reflection on God's blessings in our life...offers us a guarantee that grace is at work in us and spurs us on to an ever greater faith and an attitude of trustful poverty." Quoting St. Joan of Arc, the *Catechism* portrays the attitude that this engenders: "Asked if she knew that she was in God's grace, she replied: 'If I am not, may it please God to put me in it; if I am, may it please God to keep me there'" (*CCC* 2005).

Despite doctrinal disagreements with Catholics on this issue, Evangelicals can well understand that the beginnings of grace, manifesting "saving faith" in their perspective, serve to deepen faith as dependence on God for the living of the Christian life. As we await the promised fulfillment of the coming of God's kingdom, the promise of the world's perfection in God nurtures faith and hope with an assurance that transcends any subjective experience. To quote again section 2005 of the *Catechism*, "...grace *escapes our experience* and cannot be known except by faith." The work of the Spirit, evangelical assurance, and eschatological hope combine to anchor and empower Christian witness in its service of the Gospel.

Evangelical Biblical Ethics and Catholic Ethics within the Tradition of Theological Reflection

Morality or ethics is often expected to be the common ground that Christians share despite their denominational differences. In fact, it is probably more the case today than ever that practical alliances across ecclesiastical lines in the interest of a moral perspective in culture and society discover their common ground on the basis of the liberal or conservative sensibilities they share. Maybe a liberal Catholic and Methodist have more in common with each other than they do with their conservative counterparts in their respective churches. No doubt observers of the relationship between religion and politics will take note that the efforts of the religious right to bring Catholics and Evangelicals/Fundamentalists together are not that dissimilar from the efforts of the religious left to forge a common front between liberal Protestants and Catholics in the 1960s and beyond. To view matters strictly with these sociopolitical lenses would be a disservice to the theological dialogue and mutual understanding that we are seeking to establish. Therefore, we turn to more long-standing classical issues that arise between Evangelicals and Catholics on this important matter.

Similar to much of what we have already covered, the differences between these two Christian communions revolve around the importance of tradition for Catholics. Additionally, especially in the area of ethics, Catholics have historically given a significant place to philosophical reason and natural law. A good example would be the manner in which Thomas Aquinas blended both the divine revelation of Scripture with his reading of Aristotle to exposit the moral virtues that should exemplify the Christian life. Evangelicals, on the other hand, have focused more on the development of a biblical ethics, one that can be directly derived from God's revelation in Scripture. While not ignoring the role of reason, they have sought an explicit biblical foundation as the basis for moral guidance. While Catholic morality tended to negotiate the relationship between nature and grace, between what our human nature required and what God communicated through the incarnation and redemption, Protestant ethics kept trying to think through the relationship between Law and Gospel, between the commands and prohibitions of Scripture and the offer of salvation as a free gift. But all of this takes place at sophisticated theological levels. What about your average believer?

Indeed it all seems to boil down to two questions that the Evangelical and Catholic Christian respectively ask. What does the Bible say? What does the church teach? Both stress the importance of conscience; the Evangelical by way of personally investigating the Bible on such matters, and the Catholic by forming one's conscience through church teaching and reflecting prayerfully about the particularities of a moral decision. In more recent years both sides have come to appreciate aspects that the other has traditionally emphasized. Evangelicals are aware of thinking through issues in morality, and Catholics have been much more explicit about the biblical foundations for Catholic moral and social teaching. Witness the extensive biblical portions of the U.S. bishops' pastoral letters on peace and economic justice promulgated during the 1980s.

More to the point, Evangelical-Catholic dialogue on ethics now emphasizes the contextualization of morality and ethics within the framework of conversion to Jesus Christ. Here Evangelicals will speak of continual conversion (as articulated for Catholics above) and Catholics will stress the necessity of encountering and following Christ (similar to the personal relationship with Christ that Evangelicals have always stressed). Discipleship of Jesus Christ is perhaps the most ecumenical model for Christian ethics and morality. Catholics will always maintain, however, that reflection on such discipleship is an ecclesial event, taken within the tradition of Catholic thought as it has attempted to respond to God's Word amid its hospitality to all things human throughout the centuries. Evangelicals can discover that the reception of biblical truth over the ages represents a rich resource for faithful response to God's Word in the present.

Sacraments and Sacramentals as Means of Grace, and Understood within the Context of Conversion to Jesus Christ

Despite the efforts of many Evangelical theologians to speak of a Catholic Evangelicalism in which tradition, sacraments, and spirituality are integrated with "biblical faith," many Evangelicals remain fairly "low church" in their practice and appreciation of the sacraments. Many, for example, in the Baptist traditions understand them as "ordinances" to be practiced in obedience to Christ and that symbolically represent or confirm an important dimension of the Gospel. They do not necessarily recognize them as "means of grace" by which Christ is communicated to the church in the communion of grace and the Holy Spirit. On the other hand, any Catholic representation of sacramental life in this dialogue needs to respond to the Evangelical critique that many Catholics are sacramentalized but not evangelized! How do we proceed?

First of all, many Catholics would use similar language and would therefore acknowledge the need for evangelization in Catholic parishes. This, however, would be built on a sacramental basis, not in spite of it. The RCIA programs in fact are often the most successful means of evangelization in many Catholic congregations. This does not lessen the challenge of integrating evangelization and sacramental life at all levels of parish life, including religious education, Christian formation, ministry, and service to the community.

The *Catechism* quotes *Sacrosanctum Concilium*, the Constitution on the Sacred Liturgy, in describing the Eucharist as the "summit toward which the activity of the Church is directed...and the fount from which her power flows" (*CCC* 1074). This means that the salvific presence of Jesus Christ is at the heart of the church's sacramental life, and therefore is an invitation to evangelization and conversion. From a Catholic perspective it is within the prayer and worship of the church that the sacraments are celebrated. Authentic worship includes both the priority of divine grace and the response of the worshiping community. Sacramental grace has always been dependent on the self-giving of God and is offered through the church even despite the weakness and sinfulness of the community. However, the fruitfulness of sacramental grace is dependent on the receptivity of the community's faith and love. In this respect Catholic sacramental worship at its best is a converting action that the community enacts. The liturgy promotes an ever-deepening evangelization of the church.

No doubt this ideal portrait of Catholic sacramental worship requires ongoing catechesis on the part of the church as teacher and the active faith of the priesthood of the ordained and the faithful. Indeed sacraments are sacraments of faith. As Vatican II's Constitution on the Sacred Liturgy states, they "not only presuppose faith, but…they also nourish, strengthen and express faith" (*Sacrosanctum Concilium*, no. 59) and must be "prepared for by *the word of God and by the faith* which is assent to this word" (*CCC* 1122). Conversion to Jesus Christ is the atmosphere that sacramental worship is intended to breathe. Apart from this, the rites of the liturgy still mediate grace, but they may end up like seeds that do not mature in good soil.

The Blessed Hope: Catholics and Evangelicals on the Second Coming of Christ

As already alluded to, Evangelicals hold various positions on Christian eschatology, especially in reference to the second coming of Christ. In fact, most Evangelicals agree with Catholics that, in the words of the *Catechism*, the "glorious advent of Christ" is the hope of the Christian and the church. "He will come again to judge the living and the dead." In this respect the kingdom of God is already present and yet presses on to its final fulfillment. We await a new heaven and new earth wherein the righteousness of God will dwell (2 Pet 3:13). For Catholics this has two consequences. First, there is the ecclesial dimension. The kingdom is already present in the church.

When Jesus, who had suffered the death of the cross for mankind, had risen, He appeared as the one constituted as Lord, Christ and eternal Priest, and He poured out on His disciples the Spirit promised by the Father. From this source the Church, equipped with the gifts of its Founder and faithfully guarding His precepts of charity, humility and self-sacrifice, receives the mission to proclaim and to spread among all peoples the Kingdom of Christ and of God and to be, on earth, the initial budding forth of that Kingdom. While it slowly grows, the Church strains toward the completed Kingdom and, with all its strength, hopes and desires to be united in glory with its King. (*Lumen Gentium*, no. 5)

Second, the kingdom also relates to social progress in this world and is an impetus to the church's mission in that regard.

We do not know the time for the consummation of the earth and of humanity, nor do we know how all things will be transformed. As deformed by sin, the shape of this world will pass away; but we are taught that God is preparing a new dwelling place and a new earth where justice will abide, and whose blessedness will answer and surpass all the longings for peace which spring up in the human heart. Then, with death overcome, the sons of God will be raised up in Christ, and what was sown in weakness and corruption will be invested with incorruptibility. Enduring with charity and its fruits, all that creation which God made on man's account will be unchained from the bondage of vanity.

Therefore, while we are warned that it profits a man nothing if he gain the whole world and lose himself, the expectation of a new earth must not weaken but rather stimulate our concern for cultivating this one. For here grows the body of a new human family, a body which even now is able to give some kind of foreshadowing of the new age.

Hence, while earthly progress must be carefully distinguished from the growth of Christ's kingdom, to the extent that the former can contribute to the better ordering of human society, it is of vital concern to the Kingdom of God. (*Gaudium et Spes*, no. 39)

There are many Evangelicals who express similar sentiments about the relationship between the kingdom of God to be consummated at the second coming and the life of the church and its mission in the present. However, in the popular imagination—and because many Evangelicals profess it—one has the impression that the major Evangelical focus is on the last days just before the return of Christ. This will entail severe persecution of believers, the appearance of the Antichrist, and for some, the ingathering of the Jews to the land of Israel as well as the rapture of the church, that is, its being caught to Christ in the heavens, before the "Great Tribulation" (the last seven years before the parousia). All of this is based upon the interpretation of biblical prophecy in the books of Daniel, Ezekiel, and Revelation. Needless to say, Catholics take a quite different approach to biblical apocalyptic literature and even Evangelicals differ among themselves.

What may be surprising is that Catholics also believe in an intensification of life in this world before the parousia. Although the second advent of Christ may take place at any time, it also is signified by two events that in our eschatological hope we share with many Evangelicals (without some of the particulars that some Evangelicals add to it). The *Catechism of the Catholic Church* summarizes it best:

> The glorious Messiah's coming is suspended at every moment of history until his recognition by "all Israel," for "a hardening has come upon part of Israel" in their "unbelief" toward Jesus....The "full inclusion" of the Jews in the Messiah's salvation, in the wake of "the full number of the Gentiles," will enable the People of God to achieve "the

measure of the stature of the fullness of Christ," in which "God may be all in all." (CCC 674)

* * *

Before Christ's second coming the Church must pass through a final trial that will shake the faith of many believers. The persecution that accompanies her pilgrimage on earth will unveil the "mystery of iniquity" in the form of a religious deception offering men an apparent solution to their problems at the price of apostasy from the truth. The supreme religious deception is that of the Antichrist, a pseudo-messianism by which man glorifies himself in place of God and of his Messiah come in the flesh. (*CCC* 675)

* * *

The Church will enter the glory of the kingdom only through this final Passover, when she will follow her Lord in his death and Resurrection. The kingdom will be fulfilled, then, not by a historic triumph of the Church through a progressive ascendancy, but only by God's victory over the final unleashing of evil, which will cause his Bride to come down from heaven. God's triumph over the revolt of evil will take the form of the Last Judgment after the final cosmic upheaval of this passing world. (*CCC* 677)

I have quoted liberally to impress upon Catholics that we possess a vital and dynamic eschatological hope in the second coming of Christ, something not always emphasized in Catholic homiletics and catechesis. This not only enriches Catholic life, but also serves as a point of dialogue with our Evangelical brothers and sisters.

FIVE

The Challenge of Evangelicals to Catholics

Partners in dialogue are not only interested in conveying their own positions but also internalizing how the positions of their dialogue partners may inform their own. What challenges do Evangelicals present to Catholic faith and witness? One is never the same after an authentic dialogue. How might Catholics be enriched by the Evangelical witness?

Be Evangelized, Not Just Sacramentalized

As just previously discussed, Catholic liturgical life is not just external form. It is the signification and mediation of God's self-giving that constitutes both the worship of God and the sanctification of the community. But the testimony of many former Catholics who have joined Evangelical congregations that they have encountered Jesus Christ for the first time or in a new way—usually expressed as a personal relationship with Jesus Christ—cannot be discounted, ignored, or dismissed for its theological limitations. Rather, it should spur Catholic evangelization efforts, including those that are intended to raise faith-consciousness that sacramental life initiates and sustains the conversion process.

Sacramental preparation and catechesis need not be the only means of evangelization. Service, spirituality, preaching (including lay preaching where appropriate!), Christian formation and education, renewal movements, prayer, devotions, and many other means can all be used for evangelization. As the Gospel continues to call and convert, a converting community will be an evangelizing community. The saving encounter with Jesus Christ includes the "personal" dimension and much more. Without that dimension, however, many Catholics will discover God somewhere else and Evangelicals are more than willing to oblige. To a community whose hearts are united in a reverential familiarity with the Lord, the Evangelical challenge will not be a threat but an opportunity for bearing witness, dialogue, and growth.

Understand and Express Faith with a Biblical Foundation and Genre

Biblical and liturgical renewal coincided in the path toward Vatican II and continues in the contemporary and future church. The need for this renewal to permeate the lives and language of the faithful (not to the exclusion of tradition) is even more poignant in the United States, where biblical images and metaphors so inform our culture and religious expression. First of all, Catholics can be made familiar with how much the Bible permeates, even saturates, the liturgical and sacramental life of the church. It is always an education for Evangelicals to discover this. Too often they think that biblical witness has been smothered by tradition rather than expressed through it. But something still does remain as a challenge.

Faithful and spiritually active Catholics tend to pray with the Bible while Evangelicals prefer to study it. In other words, Bible study is a regular part of Protestant church life while the Catholic experience of the Scriptures has been primarily in the context of prayer, liturgical and contemplative. It would not harm, and would certainly enrich, Catholic life to introduce Bible study as a dimension of our spiritual diet. Many parishes already promote regular adult Bible studies and the habit of personal Bible study need not be seen as a threat to tradition or the authority of the magisterium. More familiarity with the Scriptures will help Catholics express their faith in terms that Evangelicals can understand, even if they do not agree. Also, in face of the claims by some Evangelicals/Fundamentalists to believe and practice only what the Bible says (without a hint of theological interpretation!), a Catholic who knows the Bible will be able to soften the scope of such claims in order to communicate Catholic faith and establish a basis for Christian fellowship.

Discover a Catholic Way of Witness That Brings People to Faith in Jesus Christ

Where Evangelicals and Catholics differ the most in style has to do with the manner of our witness to Christ. Testimony to Christ, being able to lead one to Christ as Savior, speaking of one's experience with Christ are all common to the Evangelical way of living the Christian life. While not all Evangelicals are evangelists in the style of a Billy Graham, all of them are nevertheless expected to be able to share their own stories and the basics of Christian faith in order to assist others in encountering Christ as Savior. Certainly, this is not the norm among Catholics.

Although we are not suggesting that the manner in which Evangelicals evangelize is appropriate for Catholics—in fact, the comprehensive approach of RCIA hesitates at the immediacy of some Evangelical conversions—we do believe that their zeal for Christ may be an encouragement for us to develop new paths in evangelization. Here we are challenged at diocesan, parochial, and personal levels of response, which is really a response to the Lord, his call in our lives, and our mission as "church." Each of these is being pursued in the life of the church. Catholics often simply need to find out what is taking place in the church, and they will discover the riches of Christ present and active in various ministries and charisms.

The idea of evangelization also seems to have caught the attention of our two most recent popes. John Paul II often spoke of the "new evangelization." Benedict XVI has now established a new Roman dicastery: the Pontifical Council for Promoting the New Evangelization. In doing so, he exhorted: "Hence, the mission of evangelization, a continuation of the work desired by the Lord Jesus, is necessary for the Church: it cannot be overlooked; it is an expression of her very nature" (Apostolic Letter *Ubicumque et Semper*).

Without discounting what I have just said, we are considering a challenge, one that I now propose. How might we nurture and assist the facility of Catholic Christians to share their faith and to do so in such a way that it is clear that their testimony reveals Jesus Christ? The richness of Catholicism allows for a variety of charisms (contemplative, active, lay, religious, etc.), all of which are anchored in the paschal mystery that the eucharistic liturgy celebrates. Our baptismal call to share in the trinitarian life of God can take shape in a variety of ways. Thus we are not interested in any monolithic solutions. How can bishops, priests, deacons, religious, spiritual directors, lay ministers, and others who exercise ministry and pastoral care in the church promote the formation of evangelistic apostolates for the future? It all comes down to whether one can share the Gospel of Jesus Christ with another out of the divine love that mission embodies.

Live the Church as a Community of Disciples, as a House of Conversion

Various models of church life have been proposed by theologians in order to live out the reality of the church. Examples familiar to Catholicism include the perfect society, the mystical body of Christ, the servant of the Lord, the people of God. Jesuit theologian Avery Cardinal Dulles suggested a model of the church as a community of disciples. I have already alluded to the spiritual vitality that many Evangelical congregations display. Many Catholic parishes do as well. But it is certainly a challenge for any congregation to consider the call to active discipleship in one's life, family, community, and nation.

A community of disciples presumes that the call to follow Jesus is at the heart of mission and of being "church." It also entails that continual call to conversion that is descriptive of the Catholic experience of grace and its operation in human life. The church as a house of conversion to Jesus Christ and a way of discipleship in following him is both Catholic and Evangelical. What could be a clearer witness to the Gospel of salvation so prized by Evangelicals than a multifaceted witness to the transformative effects of grace, which is nothing but God's love known in Christ through the power of the Holy Spirit? In this sense true Evangelicalism (the Gospel as primary) requires a true Catholic sensibility (the whole Gospel for all aspects of humanity everywhere).

Six

What Evangelicals Might Learn from Catholics

Our dialogue does not end only with what we can learn. We also have something to contribute to our partners in Christ. They may not become Catholic (which is not the goal of dialogue anyway), but they may be better Evangelicals. Evangelicals who nurture a catholic sensibility can only contribute to the cause of Jesus Christ and maybe even envision themselves as collaborators with Catholics rather than as competitors.

The Importance of Church,
Local and Universal

It would be a misrepresentation of Evangelicals to suggest that church is not important to them, especially when some are in church three or more times a week. Worship services, Bible studies, prayer meetings, and mission outreach characterize many an Evangelical congregation. What I am suggesting, however, is that visible organic unity is an important aspect of our witness to Christ in the world. Evangelicals are often content with the spiritual unity of Christians rather than their concrete visible ecclesial unity. They settle in good Reformation tradition (that of John Calvin, specifically) for the unity of the invisible church, that is, all those who are true regenerate believers. This, in fact, is no small thing. Because of their spiritual unity Evangelicals, other than separatist Fundamentalists, are noted for many cooperative ventures in mission and evangelism despite their separate denominational affiliations.

Evangelicals, it is true, have not been that enthusiastic about ecumenism, suspicious as they are of mainstream Protestantism as having forsaken the Gospel. Traditionally they have set up their own alternative organizations like the National Association of Evangelicals and the World Evangelical Alliance. Nevertheless, the unity of the church is something for which Christ prayed (John 17:23), and its disunity serves as a counterwitness to the Gospel. Is it really sufficient for an incarnational God to be content with our spiritual unity, whereas in the practical life of the church a lived unity would be a much more powerful witness to Christ? Additionally, the connection between the local and universal church again witnesses to the apostolic bonds that unite the church and emphasize the bond of a common underlying universal mission.

Another important contribution to which Catholics bear witness is the ecclesiality of the faith and the Christian life. Evangelicals have been traditionally critical of Catholic witness to the mediation of the church in our encounter with Christ. It is as if one had to choose the church or Christ! Without assuming that Evangelicals will become high church and sacramental, it is well worth emphasizing that no encounter with Christ is individualistic, although it is deeply personal. Christ present among his people is formative for Christian life. An awareness of how this may even be structured in certain ways can only contribute to Evangelical freedom, a great concern in their thinking. To recognize how Christ's self-giving is always present in the church is not to exchange a personal relationship with him for an external one. Rather the reciprocity between the personal and the communal reveals not only Christ's relationship with us but also his relationality to the Father and the Holy Spirit in the life of the church and the world, without which the fullness of Christ could not be known and communicated.

Worship as Rite and Ritual

Attention to worship is actually a genuine concern of some contemporary Evangelicals. While historically committed to the priesthood of all believers (no separate clerical state here!), Evangelical training has, in the words of one Evangelical, "emptied Sunday's worship hour of God's majesty and mystery."[3] With an emphasis upon expository preaching as the mainstay of worship, some Evangelicals are questioning whether the more liturgical and sacramental traditions have something to offer. A Catholic response would readily admit that we require our own renewal in the liturgy of the Word (especially preaching!) but would also acknowledge that attendance to rites and ritual (as distinct from just following the rubrics in a mechanistic manner) is essential to our engagement with God in worship. What appears as mere repetition to outsiders is in fact a reverential intimacy with God that calls for deeper levels of appropriation and (here it is again) conversion.

The invitation that Catholics extend to Evangelicals in the area of worship is to take seriously the incarnational aspects of worship. The inclusion of the material and the bodily as well as walking with the Lord through liturgical time while celebrating the history of salvation establishes the community of faith in the rhythm of the divine mystery, which has extended itself to us in love. Space, time, color, smells, touch, movement, art, and music all figure in the worship of God. Many Evangelicals are not adverse to this. But it is time that the auditorium and stage, which are beginning to displace even traditional Protestant sanctuary decor, yield to the wisdom of the tradition before worship becomes banal and, at worse, a form of entertainment.

Conversion as Process

Here we will not attempt to change Evangelical doctrine on justification and sanctification. Rather we shall emphasize that Evangelicals may profit by understanding that the conversion event is also a conversion process that encompasses everyday Christian life. By this I do not mean the repetition of a "decision for Christ." An overemphasis on "decisionism" has been the subject of criticism by many an Evangelical. Rather, our true emptiness before God (We can't save ourselves; Evangelicals willingly acknowledge this.) elicits our trust in God and enables our cooperation with the Holy Spirit.

Conversion is always a turning to God in which faith is active. The activity of faith is not a terminus; it proceeds through love and is deepened by love. As the medieval scholastics articulated, faith is formed by love. Continual conversion and conversion as a process is growth in love. How love informs the Christian life is the key to this Catholic contribution. Love is both gift and participation. There is no danger of "works-righteousness" since the assimilation of the gift is the maturation of the creature's own response for which God longs. In this respect sanctification as continual conversion does not measure progress as something we can hold up before God as our own accomplishment, but is simply seeking to plumb the depths of divine love in which we already now share.

The Significance of Contemplation, Prayer, and Discernment

Finally, as many Evangelicals have discovered, the long history of Catholic spirituality and prayer not only is a treasure of wisdom but also a present resource for guidance and discernment. Much Evangelical prayer focuses on intercession with some praise and worship (especially in pentecostal/charismatic circles). Contemplative attention to God and discernment of graced movements in one's affectivity have not always been strong suits with Evangelicals. Many Catholics have been nurtured in both these traditions (e.g., monastic and Ignatian prayer respectively). How might Evangelicals profit?

Key to Evangelical piety is their personal relationship with Christ. To take just one example of Catholic spirituality, namely, Ignatian spirituality (based on the *Spiritual Exercises* of St. Ignatius Loyola, the founder of the Jesuits), the prospect of encountering Christ and following him in service and in awareness of his will for one's life is the focus of prayer and discernment. Familiarity with the Lord and living in his presence (for God is found in all things) is the hallmark of this tradition. Other traditions in spirituality likewise foster their own particular charisms and ways of living in the Spirit. On the one hand then, Catholics are not strangers to a personal relationship with Christ (as well as its sacramental expression in the Eucharist). Witness this marvelous introduction to part 4 of the *Catechism of the Catholic Church* on Christian prayer.

> This mystery [of the faith], then, requires that the faithful believe in it, that they celebrate it, and that they live from it in a vital and personal relationship with the living and true God. This relationship is prayer. (*CCC* 2558)

On the other hand, this personal relationship extends far beyond a decision for salvation, as the best of Evangelicals clearly acknowledge. Sharing our communion in Christ provides for Evangelicals a sense for how this relationship extends into areas of life, practical and affective, intellectual and volitional, as well as social and cultural, which imply the total conversion of the human person. The cultivation of prayer and intimacy with God may be the best place to dialogue with Evangelicals. If this should be the case, the fruit of dialogue will certainly contribute to a church that is holy and is being made holy, all the while displaying the spousal love of its Lord.

Epilogue

It is the hope of this book to foster a dialogical relationship between Catholics and Evangelicals. This has not always been the case between our two traditions. In fact, in some quarters we are witnessing increasing tension. This is especially true where Evangelicals (especially Pentecostals) have made significant inroads among traditionally Catholic populations throughout Latin America and among U.S. Hispanics. When this has involved unethical proselytizing tactics, Catholics are rightly offended. In fact, there is a valid distinction between proselytism and evangelization. Misrepresentations of Catholicism as well as targeting practicing Catholics for evangelism are suspect. The area becomes a little gray when we are speaking of nominal Catholics or virtually "unchurched" people. The enthusiasm behind much Evangelical witness is simply to share the good news of the Gospel with those who appear untouched by it.

The fourth phase of the international dialogue between Pentecostals and the Pontifical Council for Promoting Christian Unity (1990–97) produced a final report entitled *Evangelization, Proselytism, and Common Witness*. Facing the issue head on, the report attempts to dialogue on the basis of mutual understanding and trust based on "two useful principles: [1] we cannot do what conscience forbids; [2] we can do together what conscience permits in the area of common witness" (no. 127).[4]

This will require profound and respectful engagement on many of the issues that we have discussed. May it be the case (and our prayer) that Catholics and Evangelicals can move toward cooperation rather than competition.

Notes

1. Although it should be said that much of the Evangelical support for the "religious right," e.g., the Moral Majority and the Christian Coalition of the 1980s and 1990s, came from premillennialists. Their political activism was motivated by the perception that the American public square and body politic had departed from biblical morality.

2. Richard Lints, *The Fabric of Theology: A Prolegomenon to Evangelical Theology* (Grand Rapids: Eerdmans, 1993), 49.

3. Gary M. Burge, "Are Evangelicals Missing God at Church?" *Christianity Today* 41, no. 11 (1997): 22.

4. Two paragraphs in particular are worth quoting:

No. 94. All Christians have the right to bear witness to the Gospel before all people, including other Christians. Such witness may legitimately involve the persuasive proclamation of the Gospel in such a way as to bring people to faith in Jesus Christ or to commit themselves more deeply to Him within the context of their own church. The legitimate proclamation of the Gospel will bear the marks of Christian love (cf. 1 Cor 13). It will never seek its own selfish ends by using the opportunity to speak against or in any way denigrate another Christian community, or to suggest or encourage a change in someone's Christian affiliation. Both the Pentecostal and Catholic members of this Dialogue view as proselytism such selfish actions as an illegitimate use of persuasive power. Proselytism must be sharply distinguished from the legitimate act of persuasively presenting the Gospel. Proselytism must be avoided.

No. 95. At the same time we acknowledge that if a Christian, after hearing a legitimate presentation of the Gospel, freely chooses to join a different Christian community it should not automatically be concluded that such a transfer is the result of proselytism.